august 2003

P9-DED-595

Dear Grace,
    Welcome to the World! We hope
you enjoy this book by our cousin,
Laura Duksta. It's all about LOVE!

                Best wishes always,
                Christina, Charlie,
                Thomas & Louis
                    Benoit

I LOVE YOU MORE

By Laura Duksta

Illustrated by Karen Keesler

Together We Are
Hippie and The Bald Chick

www.Hippieandthebaldchick.com

Keep
Shining
Laura
Duksta

A Big THANK YOU
to my MOM, Nana Pota, Grandma Anne and my sister Lynn
for helping to create my awesome family.
And to my nieces and nephews, TYLER, Michaela, CJ and Myranda
for adding so much to it. Good Looking Out Universe!
Love Always,
Auntie Laura

To my mom,
Who has stood by me with enormous patience and love
throughout all of my life's adventures
&
To Ferny,
Who reminds me not to forget my childlike dreams....
Hey You later!
Karen

Library of Congress CIP 2001095313
ISBN 0-9714403-0-1 $15.95

Editor: Laura Duksta
Illustration: Karen Keesler
Cover Design and Layout: Kelly Harris
Book Production: Pacific Rim
Printed in Hong Kong
Third Edition
Printed on partially recycled paper

I SHINE, INC
3760 E 6th Avenue
Hialeah, FL 33013

All the darkness in the world cannot dim the light of a single candle.
- Author Unknown

Keep shining
I Shine Inc.
Publishers

I LOVE YOU MORE

Walking outdoors one day
a little boy turned to his mother
and asked,
"Mommy, just how much
do you love me?"

Surprised at the question
but with no delay,
she replied with a smile...

I love you higher
than the highest
bird ever flew.

I love you taller
than the tallest
tree ever grew.

I love you longer
than the longest
path ever wound.

I love you prettier
than the prettiest
flower ever found.

I love you deeper
than the deepest
fish ever swam.

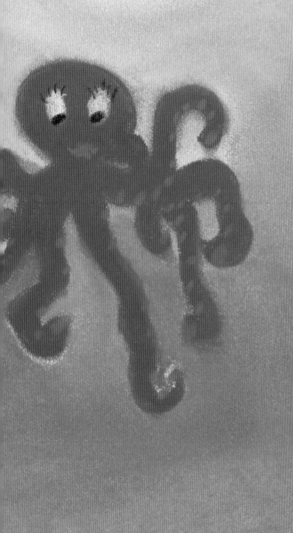

I love you stronger than the strongest big river dam.

I love you mightier
than the mightiest
wind ever blew.

I love you fuller
than the fullest
moon you ever knew.

I love you brighter
than the brightest
star ever shone.

I love you more,
so much more than
you've ever known.

Then she wrapped her
arms around him
with all the love that she had
and he felt it all surround him
when he gently whispered,
"know what mommy?..."

I love you more!

NG IN THE WHOLE WIDE WORLD. I LOVE YOU MORE THAN ANYT

NG IN THE WHOLE WIDE WORLD. I LOVE YOU MORE THAN ANYT

I love you more!

Then he wrapped his
arms around her
with all the love that he had
and she felt it all surround her
when she gently whispered,
"know what son? ..."

I love you more,
so much more
than you've ever known.

I love you taller
than the tallest
giraffe ever grown.

I love you louder
than the loudest
rocket ship ever blasted.

I love you longer
than the longest
lollipop ever lasted.

I love you sweeter than the sweetest song ever sung.

I love you higher
than the highest
swing ever swung.

I love you freer
than the freest
kite ever flown.

I love you bigger
than the biggest
bubble ever blown.

I love you further than the furthest frog ever leaped.

I love you quieter
than the quietest
caterpillar ever creeped.

Walking along a path one day,
a mother turned to her son
and asked,
"So, just how much
do you love me?"

Ready for the question,
the little boy took her hand
and began ....

I LOVE YOU MORE